GREAT BRITONS

ARTISTS

Ann Kramer

FRANKLIN WATTS

LONDON•SYDNEY

First published in 2007 by
Franklin Watts

Franklin Watts
338 Euston Road
London NW1 3BH

Franklin Watts Australia
Level 17/207 Kent Street
Sydney, NSW 2000

A CIP catalogue record for
this book is available from
the British Library.

Dewey number: 709.2241

ISBN: 978 0 7496 7472 4

Printed in China

Franklin Watts is a division
of Hachette Children's
Books.

Designer: Thomas Keenes
Art Director: Jonathan Hair
Editor: Sarah Ridley
Editor-in-Chief:
John C. Miles
Picture Research:
Diana Morris

Picture credits:
Alinari/Topfoto: 41. Ashley
Cooper/Corbis: 45. Mary
Evans Picture Library: 7,
11, 16-17. John
Hedgecoe/Topfoto: 39.
HIP/Topfoto: 9. Jeff
Mitchell/Reuters/Corbis:
front cover, 42.
Picturepoint/Topham: 12,
20, 23, 31, 35. Roger-
Viollet/Topfoto: 15, 36.
Ann Ronan Picture
library/HIP/Topfoto: 19, 26,
29. Topfoto: 25.
UPP/Topfoto: 32.

Every attempt has been made to
clear copyright. Should there be
any inadvertent omission please
apply to the publisher for
rectification.

CONTENTS

INTRODUCTION

This book contains biographies of 20 outstanding British artists. They are all painters or sculptors and have been chosen because they were either born in Britain, or became British. They have also been chosen because, from Nicholas Hilliard in the 16th century through to Damien Hirst in the 21st century, each of them has made a significant contribution to the history of British art.

The book begins in the 16th century. There had been art in Britain before that time. Monks produced exquisite illustrated manuscripts in the late 6th century, for instance. There is also a beautiful piece of medieval art, the *Wilton Diptych*, that dates back to the 1390s. It was almost definitely made in England, as a portable altarpiece for King Richard II. However, the artist may have been French.

Continental artists dominated art in Britain for many years. It was not really until the Tudor period that the first British-born artists were recognised, which is why this book begins then. It was around this time too that art ceased to be entirely religious and became what has been described as 'domestic' art, art for personal use. At first only the very rich and famous could commission and enjoy art. It was not until much later that the British public could visit exhibitions to see the work of more popular British artists.

This book is not a history of British art; it is about the men and women who made British art. But the biographies are arranged chronologically so that reading through them you will not only learn about artists' lives, you will also see how British art changed and evolved.

You, of course, will have your own favourite artists, and will wonder why some of them are not in this book. A list such as this is always personal, and can always be changed with good reason. But it is true to say that each and every person in this book influenced British art in one way or another, and has left their mark for future generations to study, and admire. 🏴

NICHOLAS HILLIARD
MINIATURIST PAINTER

BORN Exeter, c. 1547
DIED London, 1619
AGE about 72 years

Nicholas Hilliard was the first English-born painter to achieve recognition in his lifetime. He is famous for exquisite miniature paintings, some of which are not much larger than 5 cm by 5 cm.

Hilliard trained as a goldsmith in London. No one knows quite when he took up painting but his earliest known miniatures date back to about 1560. In about 1570 he was appointed miniature painter to Queen Elizabeth I. He made many portraits of her, and of other leading Elizabethans, including Sir Walter Raleigh and Sir Francis Drake. While some portrait painters simply reduced larger paintings down to a small size, Hilliard worked in miniature, producing delicate and highly-detailed tiny masterpieces, such as *An Unknown Man Against a Background of Flames* (c.1588), shown right.

The art of miniature painting was known as 'limning', a word that came from illumination. Hilliard wrote a book on the subject, *Treatise on the Arte of Limning* (c.1600). He described his method of working – he avoided shadows, for instance – and said that the great Flemish portrait painter Hans Holbein (1517-84), who worked in England for many years, had influenced his approach. Hilliard's work was popular with the nobility. The Elizabethans liked miniatures. They put them into jewelled lockets and gave them to loved ones to wear. Sometimes ambassadors, official messengers of the queen, took

Portrait painters

There were no cameras in the 16th century. Instead, royalty and the nobility had portraits painted to display their importance. **ANTHONY VAN DYCK** (1599-1641) was an outstanding portrait painter. Born in Holland, he lived in England for more than 13 years. He was court painter to King Charles I and influenced English art profoundly. **MARY BEALE** (1633-99) was a less skilled portrait painter but the first English woman to be recognised publicly as an artist.

Hilliard specialised in portraits such as this one (shown much larger than actual size).

miniature portraits of royalty with them when they travelled abroad. Hilliard also worked as a jeweller and goldsmith and in 1584 designed Queen Elizabeth's Great Seal, which she used to sign documents and letters. Despite his popularity, he often had financial problems, and on one occasion was imprisoned for debt. 🇬🇧

JAMES THORNHILL
DECORATIVE ARTIST

BORN Dorset,
25 July 1675
DIED Dorset,
13 May 1734
AGE 58 years

Decorative art was popular during the late 17th and early 18th centuries. Wealthy landowners paid artists to paint huge paintings on the walls and ceilings of their homes. Most decorative artists were Italian or French; James Thornhill was the exception.

An ambitious man, Thornhill learnt the techniques of the French and Italian decorative artists and challenged them, becoming the leading English decorative artist of the time. He was the first English-born artist to be knighted.

In 1706 Thornhill decorated the Sabine Hall at Chatsworth House, Derbyshire. Later he beat off foreign competition to win commissions to decorate the Upper and Lower Halls at Greenwich Hospital for Seamen (1707-25) and the interior of the dome of St Paul's Cathedral, London (1715-17). Thornhill painted with oil paints, straight onto plaster. His ceiling at Greenwich was the most ambitious and successful decorative project in England. A massive fresco, it showed King William and Queen Mary.
He decorated the dome of St Paul's with eight spectacular scenes from the life of Saint Paul.

Thornhill was appointed history painter to George I and was knighted in 1720.

Grinling Gibbons

GRINLING GIBBONS (1648-1721) was a decorative artist who worked in wood. He is considered to be the finest English wood carver of all time. He worked mainly in limewood and carved distinctive and lifelike cascades of fruit, leaves, flowers, birds and animals. He worked on St Paul's Cathedral, London churches and country houses. His work survives in Petworth House (Sussex), Sudbury Hall (Derbyshire) and Windsor Castle. He was born in the Netherlands, possibly to an English father, and moved to England in about 1667. King Charles II admired his work and commissioned him frequently.

He ran his own private painting academy where William Hogarth was one of his pupils. Hogarth married Thornhill's daughter and went on to become a great artist himself. 🇬🇧

The interior of the dome in St Paul's Cathedral, London, decorated by James Thornhill.

WILLIAM HOGARTH
SATIRICAL PAINTER AND ENGRAVER

BORN London,
10 November 1697
DIED London,
25 October 1764
AGE 66 years

William Hogarth was the most important English painter in the first half of the 18th century. His work was original and distinctive. He produced sequences of between four to six detailed and humorous paintings that told a moral tale. They could be 'read' like an unfolding story.

This picture from Marriage à la Mode *shows a young noble couple after a night-long party.*

Hogarth trained as a silver engraver and, by 1720, had set up his own business in London. He first made his name painting group portraits, known as conversation pieces. He then went on to the work for which he is best known – his political satires (paintings that ridiculed society). One of the earliest was a six-painting work, *A Harlot's Progress* (1732). This showed the downfall of an innocent country girl who arrived in London and was corrupted. In 1743, he poked fun at the rich, vain and corrupt in wealthy society in his paintings

Marriage à la Mode. Other work included *The Rake's Progress* (1733-35) and *Gin Lane* (1751), in which he showed the horrors of drunkenness in intricate detail. In a later series of four paintings, *The Election* (1756), he highlighted the fraud and corruption of political elections.

Most artists at that time relied on wealthy patrons for their livelihood. Hogarth broke with that tradition. He sold prints of his work directly to the public. They were popular and he made a good living. However, some dealers started selling his prints without paying him royalties. As a result, in 1735 Hogarth persuaded friends in parliament to pass a copyright law, to protect artists. In 1735 Hogarth opened his own academy, the forerunner of the Royal Academy. He became seriously ill in 1763 but continued painting until just a few months before his death. 🏴󠁧󠁢󠁥󠁮󠁧󠁿

Caricatures

English artists have been particularly good at the art of caricature – exaggerating a subject's facial features to make people laugh at them. Two of the greatest English caricaturists, who followed on from Hogarth, were **THOMAS GILLRAY** (1756-1815) and **THOMAS ROWLANDSON** (1756-1827). Gillray was particularly well known for caricaturing leading politicians.

JOSHUA REYNOLDS
PORTRAIT PAINTER AND WRITER

BORN Plympton,
Devon, 16 July 1723
DIED London,
23 February 1792
AGE 68 years

Sir Joshua Reynolds was the most influential English painter of the mid to late 18th century. A great portrait painter, he promoted the visual arts as a noble profession.

Reynolds was born the son of a clergyman and he wanted to paint from an early age. He studied painting in London and, in 1750, went to Italy where he spent more than two years studying what were known as the 'Old Masters', particularly the great Renaissance artists, such as Raphael (1483-1520). He developed a lifelong passion for their style of painting. He caught a cold while copying paintings in the Vatican that left him with permanent deafness.

From 1753 Reynolds lived in London. He worked hard and soon established himself as a successful portrait painter. He painted his subjects in classical or historical poses and was much in demand. By 1758 about 150 people were having their portraits painted by him each year, and by 1764 he was earning £6,000 a year, an enormous sum of money in those days. Reynolds knew all the successful and important artists and writers of his day. He founded a Literary Club and his friends included

Thomas Gainsborough

The 18th century was the golden age of English portrait painting. **THOMAS GAINSBOROUGH** (1727-88) was outstanding among those portrait painters. Born in Suffolk, he started copying Dutch landscapes when he was a child. He studied what was known as rococo decoration then, from 1745, began work as a portrait painter, producing sparkling portraits against imaginary landscapes. Examples include *Mr and Mrs Andrews* (1748) and *Blue Boy* (c.1770). Gainsborough also painted landscapes, including *The Harvest Wagon* (1767) and *The Watering Place* (1777), that were idyllic representations of English countryside scenes.

This 1776 self-portrait by Joshua Reynolds demonstrates his formal style of painting.

the playwright, Oliver Goldsmith, and fellow artist, Angelica Kauffman. In 1768, the Royal Academy was founded to train visual artists. It set up a summer exhibition where the very best works were displayed. Reynolds was the first president. From 1769-90 he gave annual lectures in which he talked of art as a dignified profession. He was appointed court painter and in 1769 was knighted. In 1789 Reynolds became blind in one eye and was forced to give up painting. 🇬🇧

GEORGE STUBBS
ANIMAL PAINTER AND ENGRAVER

BORN Liverpool,
   25 August 1724
DIED London,
   10 July 1806
AGE 81 years

Largely self-taught, George Stubbs was one of the most distinguished painters of his day. Many consider his paintings of horses to be some of the finest ever produced.

Stubbs was the son of a leather worker. From an early age he developed an interest in painting and anatomy (the scientific study of the body). He worked as a portrait painter and studied anatomy at the County Hospital in York. His earliest work included etchings for a textbook on midwifery.

Stubbs travelled to Rome then returned to England. He shut himself away, with his partner and child, in a farmhouse in Lincolnshire. There he spent 18 months studying, dissecting and drawing horses. In 1758 he moved to London and in 1766 published *The Anatomy of the Horse*, with engravings that he did himself. The book was immediately successful not only for its beauty but also for its scientific accuracy.

From this point Stubbs was in demand as a painter. He produced exquisite paintings of horses, either individually or in groups, and portraits of horses with

Stubbs was fascinated by the anatomy of horses, and used this knowledge in his work.

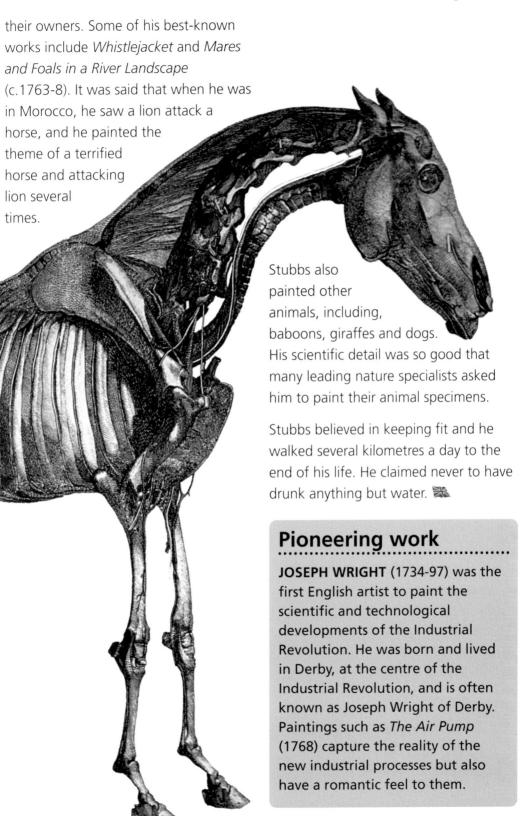

their owners. Some of his best-known works include *Whistlejacket* and *Mares and Foals in a River Landscape* (c.1763-8). It was said that when he was in Morocco, he saw a lion attack a horse, and he painted the theme of a terrified horse and attacking lion several times.

Stubbs also painted other animals, including, baboons, giraffes and dogs. His scientific detail was so good that many leading nature specialists asked him to paint their animal specimens.

Stubbs believed in keeping fit and he walked several kilometres a day to the end of his life. He claimed never to have drunk anything but water. 🇬🇧

Pioneering work

JOSEPH WRIGHT (1734-97) was the first English artist to paint the scientific and technological developments of the Industrial Revolution. He was born and lived in Derby, at the centre of the Industrial Revolution, and is often known as Joseph Wright of Derby. Paintings such as *The Air Pump* (1768) capture the reality of the new industrial processes but also have a romantic feel to them.

WILLIAM BLAKE
POET, PAINTER, ENGRAVER AND VISIONARY

BORN London,
28 November 1757
DIED London,
12 August 1827
AGE 69 years

Dismissed during his lifetime as eccentric and mad, William Blake is now considered an original and important British artist. He also wrote wonderful poems, which he illustrated and printed himself. A revolutionary, he questioned the importance of money and wealth as against spiritual happiness, and has inspired many artists, poets and thinkers.

Newton *was painted in watercolour by Blake in 1795. Blake rejected formality and created paintings in a fantastic, visionary style.*

Visionary artists

The artist **SAMUEL PALMER** (1805-81) was another visionary artist, also born in London. From the early 1820s he began to paint mystical landscapes, possibly because he had become intensely religious. A friend took him to meet William Blake, who encouraged Palmer and showed him examples of his own work. Palmer's painting, *Repose of the Holy Family* (1824-25), was strongly influenced by William Blake. In turn, Palmer's work had a strong influence on British artist **GRAHAM SUTHERLAND** (1903-80).

Blake spent most of his life in London. His mother taught him at home and his parents encouraged his artistic talents. When he was young he claimed to have seen visions of angels and ghostly monks. He said these continued throughout his life and used them in his paintings, which is why he is known as a visionary artist.

Blake went to a drawing school for five years from the age of 10 and was then apprenticed for seven years to an engraver, James Basire. His work included making drawings for Westminster Abbey. After his apprenticeship ended, he went as a student to the Royal Academy. He hated its formal approach and soon left to set up as an engraver himself. In 1783 he married Catherine Boucher and published his first book of poems, *Poetical Sketches*. He followed this with *Songs of Innocence* (1789) and *Songs of Experience* (1794). Other works included *Jerusalem* (1804-20) and drawings and engravings for Dante's *Divine Comedy*.

Blake engraved and published his books himself, using an engraving process that he developed. He wrote his text on copper plates with pens and brushes, using an acid to etch out words and illustrations. He hand-coloured his illustrations using watercolours and stitched the pages together. He sometimes said the spirit of his dead brother Robert helped him solve technical problems. Blake rejected the traditional and very formal portraits produced by artists such as Joshua Reynolds. Instead his paintings and drawings are imaginative and dramatic, often portraying religious and mystical themes. In 1795 Blake began a series of monotypes (prints made from a design painted on glass) of images from the Bible and Shakespeare. He called them 'colour printed drawings'. They had no words with them.

Blake struggled to earn a living from his work. Despite this, his wife, Catherine, was devoted to him and was with him when he died, singing hymns.

JMW TURNER
LANDSCAPE ARTIST

BORN London,
23 April 1775
DIED London,
19 November 1851
AGE 76 years

A Romantic landscape painter, Joseph Mallard William Turner worked in watercolour and oils. He produced studies of sea, light and landscapes that have never been equalled.

Turner started painting when he was young. In 1789, at the age of 14, he became a student at the Royal Academy of Art. A year later one of his watercolours was shown in the Summer Exhibition, by then an important event in the world of art. In 1796 Turner exhibited an oil painting, *Fishermen at Sea*. From then on his paintings were shown every year.

By 1800 Turner was a leading landscape artist. He opened a private gallery and was overwhelmed by commissions for his work. He travelled frequently around Britain, France, Italy and Switzerland, seeking inspiration and filling sketchbooks with drawings that he worked up into paintings.

In his earlier paintings, Turner concentrated on capturing every detail of a landscape. As his style developed, he focused more on light, colour and movement, as seen in later paintings, such as *Snowstorm: Hannibal Crossing the Alps* (1812). Violent seas and the brilliance of sunlight fascinated Turner and featured in paintings such as *The Shipwreck of the Minotaur (1805)*. By the 1840s, his style had become freer and more abstract, filled with atmosphere rather than detail. His dramatic oil painting, *Rain, Steam and Speed* (1844), shows a train travelling over a bridge, but the impression is of movement and colour while you can hardly see any details of the train or the bridge.

John Ruskin

John Ruskin (1819-1900) was an important art critic and talented painter. Born in London into a wealthy family, he studied at Oxford University. He met Turner in 1840 and praised his work as 'true, beautiful and intellectual'. Ruskin published important books of art criticism, including *Modern Painters* (1843) and *Seven Lamps of Architecture* (1849).

Turner's Rain, Steam and Speed *depicts a train crossing a bridge in a new and dramatic way.*

Some people criticised Turner's later work as too new, unconventional and even incomplete. However, the art critic John Ruskin (1819-1900) supported his work. Turner's paintings influenced French artists, later inspiring a style known as Impressionism.

Turner never married but had two long-lasting love affairs. In later life he avoided people as much as possible. When he died, he left his paintings – 20,000 of them – to the people of Britain. He is buried in St Paul's Churchyard, next to Sir Joshua Reynolds. In 1984 an annual art award was established called the Turner Prize, after the great artist. In 2005 Turner's painting *The Fighting Temeraire* (1839), which shows a great warship being towed to the breaker's yard, was voted Britain's greatest painting in a BBC poll.

JOHN CONSTABLE
ROMANTIC LANDSCAPE PAINTER

BORN East Bergholt, Suffolk, 11 June 1776
DIED London, 31 March 1837
AGE 60 years

Landscape painting is a favourite British art form. John Constable brought a new feel and Romantic style to the subject. His paintings of parts of Suffolk, now known as 'Constable country', are among the finest landscape paintings of all time.

Constable started out in his father's milling business but wanted to be an artist. He persuaded his father to let him study at the Royal Academy of Art and in 1802 exhibited his first painting. JMW Turner was also a student but their lives and paintings were very different.

Although living in London, Constable often visited his native Suffolk to sketch. In 1809, on a visit to Suffolk, he met and fell in love with Maria Bicknell. Her family disapproved and the couple did not marry until 1816, when Constable's father died leaving him some money. By 1819 Maria had tuberculosis (a lung disease). To improve her health, the couple rented a house in Hampstead, then a village, each summer, finally moving there in 1827.

Constable painted the places he loved – Hampstead and Suffolk. He worked outside, making sketches in oil and finishing off paintings in his studio. Changing skies, moving clouds and English weather fascinated him and he captured them beautifully in his paintings.

He depicted the English countryside as he saw it but also managed to get across the emotions that nature causes. He produced some of his later work, including *View on the Stour Near Dedham* (1822) and *The Lock* (1824) on large, impressive canvases.

Romanticism

Romanticism was an artistic movement that flourished between 1750 and 1850. Artists, such as **CONSTABLE** and **TURNER**, and writers, such as **WILLIAM WORDSWORTH** (1770-1850) broke away from rigid rules. They allowed their imaginations to run free and tried to focus on conveying emotion and feelings.

A self-portrait of John Constable aged 20 displays his loose, Romantic style.

Success came late. In 1824 *The Hay Wain* (1821) was exhibited in Paris. This established him as a serious artist, although he only sold 20 paintings in his lifetime. In 1828 Maria died, leaving him with seven children. Constable continued painting but never really recovered from her death. 🇬🇧

SIR DAVID WILKIE
PORTRAIT AND GENRE PAINTER

BORN Fife, Scotland,
18 November 1785
DIED at sea near
Gibraltar, 1 June 1841
AGE 55 years

A popular artist in the first half of the 19th century, David Wilkie painted detailed scenes of daily life, known as genre paintings. He established a fashion for 'anecdotal' paintings that showed everyday events.

Born the son of a Scottish minister, Wilkie studied art in Edinburgh, and worked as a portrait painter. He observed everything around him, keeping detailed visual records in his sketchbooks. His first major painting was *Pitlessie Fair*, a study of 140 people.

In 1805 Wilkie moved to London and studied at the Royal Academy of Art.

Victorian realism

The Victorian public loved detailed realistic pictures, full of activity and incidents. **WILLIAM POWELL FRITH** (1819-1909) followed Wilkie in producing witty and detailed paintings such as *Derby Day* (1856-8) and *The Railway Station* (1862). **AUGUSTUS EGG** (1816-63) was also popular. His sombre, graphic paintings showed respectable middle-class families torn apart by drunkenness or forbidden love affairs.

Blind Man's Buff, *painted by Wilkie in 1813, is a realistic depiction of a wild game.*

His painting *Village Politicians*, shown at the 1806 Exhibition, was an instant success. Others followed, including *Village Festival* (1807), which he sold for a huge sum of money, and *Blind Man's Buff* (1813), painted for the Prince Regent.

Wilkie was now very successful and the public flocked to see his work. In 1822 when his *Chelsea Pensioners Reading the Gazette of the Battle of Waterloo* was displayed at the Royal Academy, ropes were put in front to protect the painting from the crowds. He was the first British artist to attract mass public attention.

Wilkie's health was not good. He left England in 1825 and travelled abroad for three years. His painting style changed, becoming much more powerful. The public preferred his earlier work and he lost some popularity. Even so, he was knighted in 1830. In 1840 he went to Jerusalem but died on the return journey and was buried at sea.

DANTE GABRIEL ROSSETTI
PRE-RAPHAELITE ARTIST

BORN London, England, 12 May 1828
DIED Birchington-on-Sea, Kent, 9 April 1882
AGE 53 years

Dante Gabriel Rossetti was one of a group of artists known as the Pre-Raphaelite Brotherhood. They rebelled against the Royal Academy of Art, rejecting what they saw as its lifeless and formal approach. They wanted a return to purer art forms, before (pre) the time of the artist Raphael.

Rossetti came from a talented family. His sister, Christina, was a poet, and his brother, William, was an art critic. In 1848, he and fellow artists William Holman Hunt (1827-1910) and John Everett Millais (1829-96) founded the Pre-Raphaelite Brotherhood. Early works included Rossetti's painting *The Girlhood of Mary Virgin* (1849) and Millais' *Christ in the House of His Parents* (1849-50). The novelist Charles Dickens said that their paintings were 'revolting and repulsive' but the art critic John Ruskin (see p 18) supported and praised them. The Victorian public loved their work.

The first phase of the Brotherhood ended in 1853 and Millais went his own way. Rossetti revived the group in 1856, this time with Edward Burne-Jones (1833-98) and William Morris (1834-96). Their medieval style dominated English art in the second half of the 19th century. Rossetti's life was romantic but troubled. He married his model, Elizabeth Siddal, but she

William Morris

WILLIAM MORRIS (1834-96) was a designer, artist and socialist. He believed art should be both beautiful and useful. He founded a decorating firm in 1861, producing furniture, fabrics, stained glass, wallpaper and carpets. His company was modelled on a medieval craft guild, in which craftspeople produced exquisite handcrafted products. His work was influential and led to what was known as the Arts and Crafts Movement.

The Beloved (1865-6) depicts a scene from the Song of Solomon in the Bible.

committed suicide in 1862. Consumed by guilt, he buried his poems in her grave (but later dug them up and published them) and immortalised her in paintings such as *Beata Beatrix*. He fell in love with Jane Burden, the wife of William Morris, and painted her obsessively as a goddess. In later life, Rossetti became an alcoholic and a drug addict. He kept two wombats as pets; one slept on his dining table, and may have inspired the dormouse in Lewis Carrol's book *Alice in Wonderland*. 🇬🇧

25

WALTER SICKERT
IMPRESSIONIST ARTIST

BORN Munich, Germany, 31 May 1860
DIED Bath, England, 22 January 1942
AGE 81 years

Influenced by French artists, Walter Sickert painted Impressionistic scenes of London that influenced many English artists in the years before and after World War I (1914-18). He founded what was known as the Camden Town Group.

Sickert was brought up in England. His father and grandfather were painters but he wanted to be an actor. After a brief, not very successful career, he became a student at the Slade School of Art in London. He studied with the American artist, James Whistler, and with the French Impressionist, Edgar Degas, in Paris. He spent time in Dieppe then returned to England, where he introduced the Impressionist style that he had picked up from France.

Unlike many previous artists, Sickert did not paint outdoors. He worked indoors, often painting from photographs. His favourite subjects were music halls, drab and artificially lit interiors, and shabby London street scenes, which he painted in deep rich browns in an Impressionistic way. He took elements from other artists but developed a style uniquely his own.

Sickert was a forceful, witty personality and was much liked. He married three times and was a skilled etcher and teacher, founding seven private art schools. He became fascinated by crime and painted several scenes of a notorious Camden Town murder. In recent years, some people suggested that he was Jack the Ripper, who committed gruesome and unsolved murders in London in 1888. In fact Sickert was in France at the time.

Camden Town Group

In 1911 Sickert set up an avant-garde group of artists known as the Camden Town Group. There were 16 artists in the group, including **WYNDHAM LEWIS** (see pp 30-31) and **AUGUSTUS JOHN** (see p 28). The group only lasted for two years but it became known for distinctive paintings of town life, in a style known as post-Impressionist that influenced other artists up to World War II (1939-45).

Walter Sickert introduced the Impressionist style of painting to England.

GWEN JOHN
PORTRAIT ARTIST

BORN Haverfordwest,
Wales, 22 June 1876
DIED Dieppe, France,
3 September 1939
AGE 63 years

Gwen John painted exquisite portraits in gentle colours. During her lifetime, she did not receive the same recognition as her brother, the artist Augustus John. Now she is seen as a major British artist.

Between 1895-8 Gwen John studied at the Slade School of Art in London. She took lessons in Paris from the American artist, James Whistler, and returned to London where she began to exhibit her work in 1899. In 1904 she moved to France, where she remained. She earned a living working as an artist's model, posing for various artists, including the sculptor Auguste Rodin (1840-1917), with whom she had a love affair.

In 1913 Gwen John became a Catholic and sought solitude. Her best-known work includes single portraits of women. She painted in a quiet, delicate style, often re-working the same image many times. She used studio models and sketched from life, on trains and in churches. She included cats in many of her works.

During her lifetime, Gwen John had only one solo exhibition, in London in 1936. Her brother, Augustus, was far more popular. He believed, however, that she was the better artist. Today, most critics agree and she is celebrated worldwide. In 2005 Tate Britain hosted a major exhibition of Gwen and Augustus John's work.

Augustus John

AUGUSTUS JOHN (1876-1961) was a far more colourful character than his sister, Gwen. They both studied art at the Slade, but by the time he was 25, he had become the most famous British artist of his day. He was known for his skilled drawings and memorable portraits of such leading writers as **GEORGE BERNARD SHAW, DYLAN THOMAS** and **JAMES JOYCE**. For a while he lived with the Roma (travelling people), painting them in *Encampment on Dartmoor* (1906). During World War I (1914-18) he accompanied Canadian forces as an official war artist.

A portrait of Gwen John painted by Ambrose McEvoy (1878-1939).

WYNDHAM LEWIS
WRITER AND ARTIST

BORN Nova Scotia,
Canada,
18 November 1882
DIED London,
7 March 1957
AGE 74 years

Wyndham Lewis pioneered abstract art in Britain. He founded Vorticism, a short-lived but dynamic art movement that had a strong impact on British art.

Born on his father's yacht off the Canadian coast, Lewis studied art in London and then Paris. He returned to England and soon became a major avant-garde artist.

From 1911 he developed a revolutionary art style that was angular and very modern, taking some elements from Cubism and Futurism. Together with his friend, the American poet Ezra Pound, he launched the Vorticist movement in 1914 and edited its magazine *Blast*.

During World War I (1914-18), Lewis served in the Royal Artillery, fighting on the Western Front. In 1917 he became an official war artist for the British and Canadian governments with the task of making a visual record of the war. His painting *A Battery Shelled* (1918) is Vorticist in style and was based on his experiences in charge of field artillery at the battle of Ypres.

After the war, Lewis concentrated on writing, producing a number of novels

The Vorticists

Vorticism only lasted until 1915 but it had a profound impact on British art. The American poet **EZRA POUND** (1885-1972) gave the movement its name. The Vorticist style, which Lewis developed, was harsh, machine-like and angular, reflecting the machine world. Other Vorticists included British artists **DAVID BOMBERG** (1890-1957), **JESSICA DISMORR** (1885-1939) and **HELEN SAUNDERS** (1885-1963), and American-born sculptor **JACOB EPSTEIN** (1880-1959). The Vorticists produced their own magazine, *Blast*. There were only two issues but the magazine's appearance revolutionised graphic design. The Vorticists put on one exhibition, in 1915.

and essays. He was associated with the British Fascist Party and supported the German Nazi dictator, Adolf Hitler. As a result, many people disapproved of him. He later gave up his far-right views.

Lewis returned to painting in the late 1930s, using a more conventional style. He produced some fine portraits, including studies of the British writer Edith Sitwell and the poet TS Eliot.

Wyndham Lewis in his studio - a photograph taken in 1916.

VANESSA BELL
PAINTER AND MEMBER OF THE BLOOMSBURY GROUP

BORN London,
30 May 1879
DIED Sussex,
7 April 1961
AGE 81 years

Vanessa Bell was a leading artist in the early part of the 20th century when not many women artists were succeeding. Inspired by the post-Impressionist style, she produced abstract and colourful paintings and designs.

The daughter of the leading literary critic, Sir Leslie Stephen, Vanessa Stephen studied art in London. Her early paintings, such as *Iceland Poppies* (1908), were gentle and naturalistic. They were praised but she was not satisfied with her art style, which was soon to change dramatically.

After her parents' death, Vanessa, her brothers and sister, moved to the Bloomsbury area of London. Their house became the centre for an extraordinary and creative group of writers, artists and intellectuals, known as the Bloomsbury Group. The group, which was famous for its free and easy lifestyle, rejected Victorian values. They wanted art and life to be free and unconventional.

In 1910 one of their members, Roger Fry, (1866-1934) set up a post-Impressionist exhibition in London. It had a powerful impact on Vanessa Bell. From then on, her paintings and designs became increasingly abstract. By 1914 she was recognised as a leading modern artist.

Vanessa married Clive Bell, the art critic and poet, in 1907 and they had two sons. They had an open marriage and both had affairs. Vanessa Bell also fell in love with the artist and member of the Bloomsbury Group, Duncan Grant (1885-1978), with whom she had a daughter.

During World War I, Vanessa Bell, her children and Duncan Grant, moved to Sussex, where they rented a farmhouse, Charleston. It became a centre for many artists and writers who were frequent visitors. The 1930s and 1940s were times of tragedy. Roger Fry died, her son, Julian, was killed fighting in the Spanish Civil War, and her sister Virginia Woolf committed suicide. Vanessa painted into old age, but her paintings became less fashionable. 🎏

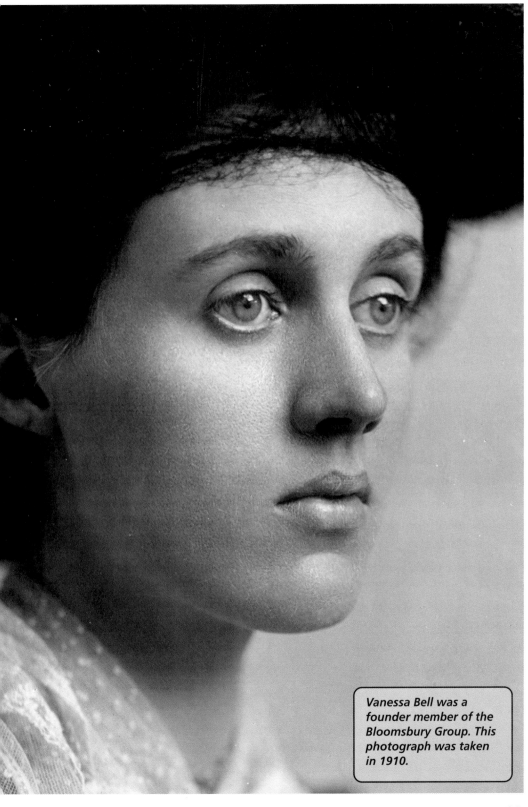

Vanessa Bell was a
founder member of the
Bloomsbury Group. This
photograph was taken
in 1910.

HENRY MOORE
SCULPTOR AND WAR ARTIST

BORN Castleford,
Yorkshire,
30 July 1898
DIED Much Hadham,
Hertfordshire,
31 August 1986
AGE 88 years

Henry Moore was a leading 20th century sculptor. His huge abstract sculptures broke with traditional forms. His work was acclaimed worldwide and has influenced many modern sculptors.

When he was eleven, Moore knew he wanted to be a sculptor, although his father, a mining engineer, wanted him to be a teacher. He fought in World War I and afterwards received an ex-serviceman's grant to study. He studied art in Leeds and at the Royal College of Art in London, where he later taught.

Moore's early works were carvings in wood and stone. He rejected the idea that sculptures should be realistic and perfect. He believed the natural features of his materials, such as grain in wood or bumps in stone, should form part of the sculpture. He admired tribal African art and Mayan sculptures and, from the 1920s, introduced their simpler and more abstract forms into his work. He moved from carving, to casting his sculptures in bronze.

Moore married Irena Radetsky, a Polish-Russian art student, and they moved to Hampstead, London,

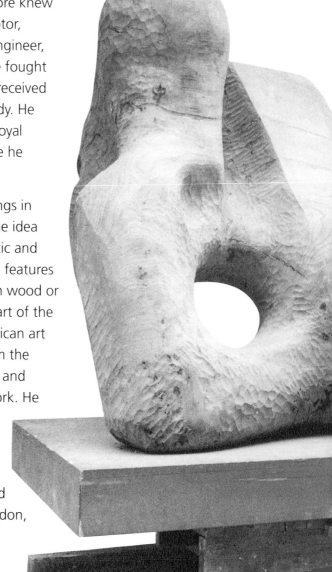

where they mixed with other avant-garde artists. He was an official war artist during World War II and his 'Shelter Drawings' of huddled people during the Blitz brought him international fame. The family moved out of London and, following his daughter's birth in 1946, Moore began working on huge, hollowed-out sculptures of family groups, particularly mothers and children. By now Moore was seen as one of the greatest living sculptors. Commissions poured in and his work was placed in many public spaces, including a massive piece in front of the UNESCO building in Paris. 🇬🇧

War artists

The British government sponsored leading British artists as official war artists to record the war for information or propaganda. War artists included **SIR STANLEY SPENCER** (1891-1959), **ERIC RAVILIOUS** (1903-42), **PAUL NASH** (1889-1946) and **DAME LAURA KNIGHT** (1877-1970), whose paintings of women munitions workers are famous. In 2006 the Imperial War Museum, London, mounted an exhibition of Henry Moore's war paintings to mark the 20th anniversary of his death.

Henry Moore poses for a photograph in his studio, c.1960.

BARBARA HEPWORTH
SCULPTOR

BORN Wakefield,
10 January 1903
DIED St Ives, Cornwall,
20 May 1975
AGE 72 years

With Henry Moore, Barbara Hepworth was a leading abstract sculptor. She studied at Leeds School of Art, where she met Moore. They were lifelong friends and often bounced ideas off each other. She also went to London's Royal College of Art.

Barbara Hepworth worked in wood and stone, carving directly into her materials, rather than producing moulds and casting, which was the traditional method. Her early work featured lifelike animals and people. In 1931 she met the artist Ben Nicholson, who later became her second husband. They were both interested in modern art. They mixed with other European abstract artists and were part of an avant-garde group of artists in London that included Henry Moore and Paul Nash.

The 7 & 5 Society

BEN NICHOLSON (1894-1982) pioneered and promoted abstract art in Britain. In 1924 he joined the 7 & 5 Society (so called because it included seven painters and five sculptors). Barbara Hepworth and Henry Moore also joined. The original aim of the 7 & 5 Society, which was founded in 1919, had been to keep alive traditional artistic values. Nicholson took the Society over, expelled the traditionalists and, in 1935, organised the first all-abstract exhibition in London.

Barbara Hepworth was an innovator (she developed new ideas). She was interested in the space around and between objects and in 1931 created *Pierced Hole*, a sculpture that included a piercing or 'hole'. It became a feature of all her work and influenced others, including Moore.

In 1939 Hepworth and Nicholson moved to the fishing village of St Ives, in Cornwall. Its dramatic scenery and beautiful light made it popular with many artists and an artists' colony developed. Hepworth loved St Ives and began producing large abstract pieces in marble and Cornish slate, and in walnut, teak and mahogany wood. Later she worked in metal, making bronze casts.

Barbara Hepworth is one of the best-known British sculptors. This photo was taken c.1968.

By the 1950s Hepworth was internationally famous. She was commissioned to do public sculptures, including *Single Form* (1963), a memorial to the UN Secretary General, Dag Hammarskjold. In 1965 she became a Dame of the British Empire. She died in a fire in her studio in 1975. 🏴󠁧󠁢󠁥󠁮󠁧󠁿

FRANCIS BACON
EXPRESSIONIST PAINTER

BORN Dublin, Ireland.
28 October 1909
DIED Madrid, Spain,
28 April 1992
AGE 82 years

A self-taught artist, Francis Bacon created powerful and disturbing images of the human figure, when most other artists were producing abstract works. His paintings were controversial but many people consider him to be the most original British artist of the 20th century.

Bacon in his studio. Throughout his life he was a controversial and brilliant figure in the art world.

Bacon's parents were English and his father was a racehorse trainer. His home life was difficult and his parents asked him to leave when he was 16. He drifted in Berlin and Paris and in 1928 arrived in London. Here, he worked as an interior designer and started painting. In 1945 his work *Three Studies for Figures at the Base of a Crucifixion* was exhibited at the Tate Gallery in London. Critics and visitors to the exhibition were shocked. The paintings showed distorted anguished human faces, and many found his work repellent. Even so, it brought him fame.

Bacon took human pain, suffering and despair as his subject matter. He worked in oils, using smeared, violent colours. Some paintings were based on his everyday life but he also worked from early photographs, films and other artists' paintings. His paintings were so new and different that the critics did not know what to make of them. Some loathed his work; others thought he was brilliant. An exhibition of 90 paintings in 1962 established him as a major artist. Another large exhibition in 1985 led to one art critic describing him as the greatest living painter. Bacon's life was as controversial as his paintings. He had many destructive homosexual love affairs and drank and gambled heavily. He destroyed many of his paintings.

Lucian Freud

Born a German Jew, **LUCIAN FREUD** (1922-) moved with his family to England to escape Nazi persecution. He became a British citizen in 1939. He is famous for his portraits, particularly his expressive paintings of nude figures. His work includes portraits of fellow artists **FRANCIS BACON** and **DAVID HOCKNEY** (see pp 40-41), and Queen Elizabeth II, in 2001. The last was criticised as unflattering. Freud says he paints people 'how they happen to be'.

DAVID HOCKNEY
POP ARTIST, PRINTMAKER AND STAGE DESIGNER

BORN Bradford,
9 July 1937

In the 1960s Pop art hit Britain, when David Hockney pioneered the new style in his paintings. Today he is famous worldwide. He has lived in the United States since the 1970s.

Hockney studied art in Bradford then at London's Royal College of Art. He was rapidly seen as the most promising student of his generation. His early Pop art paintings made his name when they were exhibited at the Young Contemporaries exhibition in 1961. Through paintings such as *We Two Boys Together Clinging* (1961), Hockney also made no secret that he was gay.

In the mid-1960s, Hockney visited the United States. He met the American Pop artist Andy Warhol in New York and then went to California. The light and brightness of California inspired some of his best-known work, vibrant blue oil paintings of swimming pools in Los Angeles, such as *A Bigger Splash* (1967). Hockney's style became less Pop and more realistic. He produced many portraits of friends, including a family portrait of the British fashion designer Ossie Clark with his wife and cat. Entitled *Mr and Mrs Clark and Percy* (1970-1), it was voted one of the most popular paintings in the UK in 2005.

Hockney is a skilled printmaker and has produced etchings for an edition of

Pop art

Pop art flourished in Britain and the United States in the 1950s and 1960s. The term 'Pop' was short for 'popular' and it was so called because Pop art used images from popular culture, such as comics, adverts, television and movies. British Pop artists included **DAVID HOCKNEY, PETER BLAKE** (1932-), who designed the cover for the Beatles' *Sergeant Pepper's Lonely Hearts Club Band*, and **RICHARD HAMILTON** (1922-). Another movement was Op art (short for Optical art) in which artists painted abstract images that appeared to move. **BRIDGET RILEY** (1931-) was the most famous British Op artist.

Grimm's *Fairy Tales*. He has designed stage sets and has experimented with new technology to produce images.

Some of his work consists of collages of faxes and photographs and he has used computer-generated images. 🇬🇧

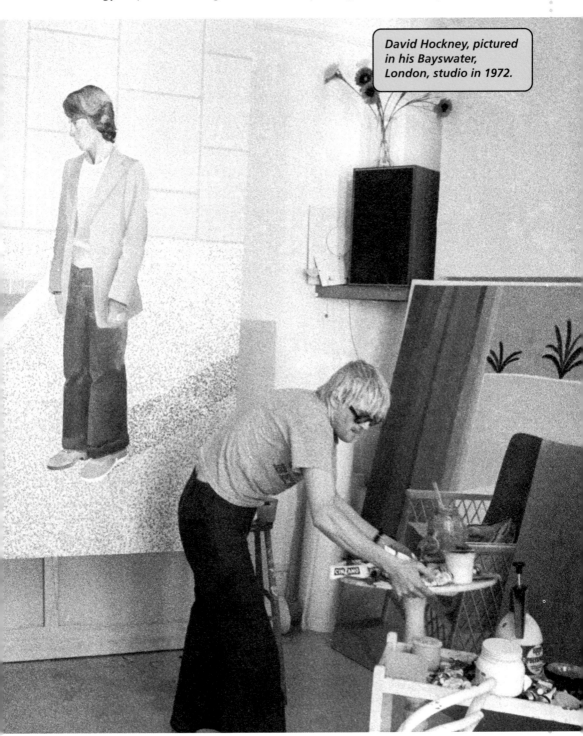

David Hockney, pictured in his Bayswater, London, studio in 1972.

ANISH KAPOOR
SCULPTOR

BORN Mumbai, India,
12 March 1954

One of a group of new and talented British sculptors, Anish Kapoor crafts abstract and sometimes mystical pieces that have been shown around the world.

Born of a Hindu mother and Jewish father, Anish Kapoor arrived in England in the early 1970s and studied art in London. He works in London, but visits India regularly. His work is influenced by Indian art and mythology as well as Western culture.

Kapoor's sculpture Marsyas filled the Turbine Hall at the Tate Modern in London.

Kapoor's sculptures tend to be simple, curved pieces. He uses natural materials, such as sandstone, marble and slate. His early work was often covered with brightly coloured dye, which he added to the sculptures and the floor around them, so they resembled mounds of coloured dye found in Indian markets. Later Kapoor produced larger sculptures out of quarried stone, often adding openings into the work.

Since the 1990s he has produced massive work, including *Taratantara* (1999), a 35-metre tall sculpture, and *Marsyas* (2002), a 150-metre sculpture made of red plastic fabric connected to steel rings, which was installed in the Turbine Hall of the Tate Modern in London. Kapoor spent nine months planning *Marsyas*, which was named after a character in Greek mythology, and it took 40 people six weeks to build it.

His other works include *Parabolic Waters* (2000), a sculpture of rapidly rotating coloured water, and *Cloud Gate* (2004), a vast sculpture. Recently he has worked on a memorial to British victims of the 9/11 terrorist bombing of New York.

New British sculpture

By the 1980s a number of new British-based sculptors were emerging, as well as Kapoor. They included **TONY CRAGG** (1949-), **GRENVILLE DAVEY** (1961-) and **RICHARD DEACON** (1949-). They worked in modern or industrial materials and many have won the Turner Prize, an annual prize given to a British visual artist under the age of 50, named after JMW Turner. Another modern British sculptor is **ANTONY GORMLEY** (1950-). He concentrates on crafting sculptures of the human body. His best-known work is *Angel of the North*, a 20-metre high steel sculpture that stands outside Gateshead, near Newcastle-upon-Tyne.

DAMIEN HIRST
CONCEPTUAL ARTIST

BORN Bristol,
7 June 1965

In 1992 an artwork consisting of a dead tiger shark floating in a tank of preserving fluid went on show. It was called the *Physical Impossibility of Death in the Mind of the Living*. The artist was Damien Hirst. His work hit the headlines and caused a massive stir. Since then Damien Hirst has been the most controversial of what are known as the Young British Artists.

Damien Hirst first found fame with his work featuring a preserved dead shark in a tank.

Hirst lived a wild life as a young man. He was often in trouble as a child and did badly at school. He managed to get to college, and studied art in Leeds and London. While he was still a student, he began to make his name when he organised an exhibition of students' work called *Freeze*. Leading art collectors and critics attended, including Charles Saatchi, who bought and promoted Hirst's work.

Death fascinated Hirst – he had worked in a mortuary when he was a student – and most of his early installation work

featured dead fish, cows and sheep. In 1995 he won the Turner Prize for an artwork consisting of a rotting cow full of maggots. Some critics were outraged and said his work could not be called art, while others thought he was the most original living artist. Hirst said he wanted to shock people. In 2003, he exhibited a dead shark with the title *A Dead Shark Isn't Art*.

Since the 1990s Hirst has become one of the most expensive artists in the world. In 2004 *Physical Impossibility* sold for £6.5 million, the second most expensive work by a living artist. (The most expensive was a piece by artist Jasper Johns.) Hirst's recent work includes sculptures and some simpler 'spot' paintings.

Young British Artists

The Young British Artists (YBAs) are a group of conceptual British artists who produce unusual and provocative work. They include painters, sculptors and installation artists. Their name comes from a 1992 exhibition called *Young British Artists*. Art collector **CHARLES SAATCHI** has promoted and shown their work in his London gallery. Key artists include **TRACEY EMIN, SARAH LUCAS**, the **CHAPMAN BROTHERS** (Jake and Dino) and **RACHEL WHITEREAD**.

Glossary

Abstract art Art that does not portray objects or scenes realistically but instead is made up of shapes and colours.

Altarpiece A picture or relief of a religious subject, placed in a frame behind the altar of a church.

Arts and Crafts Movement A movement in the late 19th and early 20th centuries that promoted good design and skilled hand craftsmanship.

Avant-garde Any group of artists that considers itself ahead of its time. It can also describe a movement in art or literature.

Baroque An ornamental style of European architecture and art that lasted from the mid-16th to early 18th centuries.

Commission An order given to an artist to produce a piece of art, for which he/she will be paid.

Conceptual art A type of art that is concerned to show ideas or concepts rather than depicting real objects or landscapes.

Conversation piece A type of group portrait. The paintings were usually quite small and showed a family or group of friends, often in an informal setting and sometimes in conversation. Conversation pieces were popular in the 18th century.

Cubism A style of painting that flourished in the early 20th century and revolutionised abstract art. It showed natural objects, including people, as geometric shapes seen from many angles. Artists Pablo Picasso and Georges Braque pioneered Cubism.

Engraving The process of cutting or etching images onto a hard surface. A print of an image made from an engraved plate.

Etching The process of creating an etched design or the prints made from an etched plate. Etching involves carving a design or drawing on a surface, either by using acid or a sharp tool.

Expressionism A style of painting that tries to express inner emotions, often by distorting or exaggerating features.

Fresco Painting on a wall or ceiling made by brushing watercolour onto fresh damp plaster.

Futurism An artistic movement between 1909-14 that combined elements of Cubism with vibrant colours and used repeating forms to convey the speed and energy of the modern world.

Genre A word used in art history to describe paintings that show scenes from daily life. It can also be used in a broader sense to mean a particular category of art, for instance landscape painting or portrait painting.

Gothic Architectural style popular in Western European churches and cathedrals between the 12th to 15th centuries. Included high curved ceilings, pointed arches and flying buttresses.

Great Masters See Old Masters

Impressionism An influential art movement that began in France in the 1860s. Impressionists experimented with light and fragments of colour to produce impressions of the natural world.

Installation art Usually describes one-off large pieces of artwork installed or placed in a gallery or public place. It has emerged as an art style since the 1970s.

Industrial Revolution The period in British history c. 1760-1830 when Britain started to become an industrial nation.

Landscape A painting of scenery, usually a countryside scene.

Limewood A soft light-coloured wood, very adaptable for carving.

Oil paint Paint in which oil, often linseed oil, is used as the base and as a drying medium. It is a versatile medium and can be used to produce a range of different shadings, depths and effects.

Old Masters Outstanding European artists who lived and worked between about 1500-1800. They include painters such as the Italian artists Leonardo da Vinci (1452-1519), Michelangelo (1475-1564) and Caravaggio (1573-1610) and the Dutch painter Rembrandt van Rijn (1606-1669).

Pioneer To start something new, or lead the way.

Portrait A painting of a person; can be the face or whole body.

Pre-Raphaelite Brotherhood The name given to a group of artists in the mid 19th century, including Rossetti, Holman Hunt and Millais, who were influenced by the style and simplicity of art before (pre) the Renaissance artist, Raphael (1483-1520).

Romanticism A movement in art and literature that flourished in the late 18th and early 19th centuries.

Renaissance The word 'renaissance' means 'rebirth'. It describes a period in European history from the 14th-17th centuries when great artists, writers and thinkers flourished.

Rococo A style in art and architecture that was popular in 18th century Europe. It was light, airy and graceful.

Royalties Money paid to an artist for every copy of a painting, or print of their paintings sold.

Satire Using sarcasm or heavy humour to expose corruption, wickedness or stupidity. Writers, comedians and others often use satire to expose politicians.

Watercolour Paint that is mixed with water, or a painting in watercolour.

Some useful websites

http://www.artcyclopedia.com/nationalities/British.html
This website lists all the British artists in this book, and many more.

http://www.spartacus.schoolnet.co.uk/art.htm
A history of British Art from 1600 to 1950.

http://www.tate.org.uk/
The home page of the Tate galleries.

Note to parents and teachers:
Every effort has been made by the Publishers to ensure that the websites in this book are suitable for children, that they are of the highest educational value, and that they contain no inappropriate or offensive material. However, because of the nature of the Internet, it is impossible to guarantee that the contents of these sites will not be altered. We strongly advise that Internet access is supervised by a responsible adult.

SOME PLACES TO VISIT

National Portrait Gallery, London
Many famous paintings can be seen here.

Tate Britain, London
This art gallery focuses on the work of British painters.

Tate Modern, South Bank, London
Modern art by British and international artists.

Tate Liverpool, Liverpool
Tate St Ives, Cornwall

Imperial War Museum, London
Works by British war artists.

Manchester City Art Gallery

National Gallery of Wales

Gainsborough House, Sudbury, Suffolk
The museum and art gallery in the house where Gainsborough was born.

Charleston farmhouse, Firle, East Sussex

Barbara Hepworth Museum and Sculpture Garden, St Ives, Cornwall

National Gallery of Scotland, Edinburgh

Birmingham Museum & Art Gallery, Birmingham
Largest collection of pre-Raphaelite art in the UK.

Salt's Mill, Saltaire, Yorkshire
Works by David Hockney.

Index

These are the lists of contents for each title in *Great Britons*:

LEADERS
Boudica • Alfred the Great • Richard I • Edward I • Robert Bruce
Owain Glyndwr • Henry V • Henry VIII • Elizabeth I
Oliver Cromwell • The Duke of Marlborough • Robert Walpole
Horatio Nelson • Queen Victoria • Benjamin Disraeli
William Gladstone • David Lloyd George • Winston Churchill
Clement Attlee • Margaret Thatcher

CAMPAIGNERS FOR CHANGE
John Wycliffe • John Lilburne • Thomas Paine • Mary Wollstonecraft
William Wilberforce • Elizabeth Fry • William Lovett
Edwin Chadwick • Lord Shaftesbury • Florence Nightingale
Josephine Butler • Annie Besant • James Keir Hardie • Emmeline Pankhurst
Eleanor Rathbone • Ellen Wilkinson • Lord David Pitt • Bruce Kent
Jonathon Porritt • Shami Chakrabati

NOVELISTS
Aphra Behn • Jonathan Swift • Henry Fielding • Jane Austen
Charles Dickens • The Brontë Sisters • George Eliot • Lewis Carroll
Thomas Hardy • Robert Louis Stevenson • Arthur Conan Doyle
Virginia Woolf • D H Lawrence • J R R Tolkien • George Orwell
Graham Greene • William Golding • Ian McEwan • J K Rowling
Caryl Phillips • Andrea Levy • Zadie Smith
Monica Ali • Salman Rushdie

ARTISTS
Nicholas Hilliard • James Thornhill • William Hogarth
Joshua Reynolds • George Stubbs • William Blake • J M W Turner
John Constable • David Wilkie • Dante Gabriel Rossetti
Walter Sickert • Gwen John • Wyndham Lewis • Vanessa Bell
Henry Moore • Barbara Hepworth • Francis Bacon • David Hockney
Anish Kapoor • Damien Hirst

ENGINEERS
Robert Hooke • Abraham Darby • James Watt • John MacAdam
Thomas Telford • George Cayley • George Stephenson • Robert Stephenson
Joseph Paxton • Isambard Kingdom Brunel • Henry Bessemer
Joseph Bazalgette • Joseph Whitworth • Charles Parsons • Henry Royce
Nigel Gresley • Lord Nuffield • Harry Ricardo • Frank Whittle • Norman Foster

SCIENTISTS
John Dee • Robert Boyle • Isaac Newton • Edmond Halley • William Herschel
Michael Faraday • Charles Babbage • Mary Anning • Charles Darwin
Lord Kelvin • James Clerk Maxwell • Ernest Rutherford • Joseph Rotblat
Dorothy Hodgkin • Alan Turing • Francis Crick • Stephen Hawking
John Sulston • Jocelyn Bell Burnell • Susan Greenfield

SPORTING HEROES
WG Grace • Arthur Wharton • Kitty Godfree • Roger Bannister
Stirling Moss • Jackie Stewart • Bobby Moore • George Best
Gareth Edwards • Barry Sheene • Ian Botham • Nick Faldo
Torville and Dean • Lennox Lewis • Daley Thompson • Steve Redgrave
Tanni Grey-Thompson • Kelly Holmes • David Beckham • Ellen McArthur

MUSICIANS
William Byrd • Henry Purcell • George Frideric Handel • Arthur Sullivan
Edward Elgar • Henry Wood • Ralph Vaughan Williams • Noel Coward
Michael Tippet • Benjamin Britten • Vera Lynn
John Dankworth and Cleo Laine • Jacqueline Du Pre
Eric Clapton • Andrew Lloyd Webber • Elvis Costello
Simon Rattle • The Beatles • Courtney Pine • Evelyn Glennie